Rasperry Pi

Effective method to run Spotify, Gaming Console utilizing RetroPie, WhatsApp to Send and Receive Messages, Software TensorFlow, Interface PCF8591 ADC/DAC Analog Digital Converter etc,...

CONTENTS

ACKNOWLEDGMENTS

The writer might want to recognize the diligent work of the article group in assembling this book. He might likewise want to recognize the diligent work of the Raspberry Pi Foundation and the Arduino bunch for assembling items and networks that help to make the Internet of Things increasingly open to the overall population. Yahoo for the democratization of innovation!

INTRODUCTION

The Internet of Things (IOT) is a perplexing idea comprised of numerous PCs and numerous correspondence ways. Some IOT gadgets are associated with the Internet and some are most certainly not. Some IOT gadgets structure swarms that convey among themselves. Some are intended for a solitary reason, while some are increasingly universally useful PCs. This book is intended to demonstrate to you the IOT from the back to front. By structure IOT gadgets, the per user will comprehend the essential ideas and will almost certainly develop utilizing the rudiments to make his or her very own IOT applications. These included ventures will tell the per user the best way to assemble their very own IOT ventures and to develop the models appeared. The significance of Computer Security in IOT gadgets is additionally talked about and different systems for protecting the IOT from unapproved clients or programmers. The most significant takeaway from this book is in structure the tasks yourself.

1. THE MOST EFFECTIVE METHOD TO RUN SPOTIFY ON RASPBERRY PI UTILIZING MOPIDY MUSIC SERVER

In past article, we secured different Music gushing programming projects which can be introduced on Raspberry Pi. Here we will pick one of them and introduce it on Raspberry Pi. Since we secured the establishment of media servers like Kodi and Plex in our past instructional exercises, I feel this time, we should turn the spotlight towards the audiophiles and spread introducing one of the music servers on the Raspberry Pi.

In the event that you resemble me, you likely utilize your Raspberry Pi(s) for more than one undertaking all things considered introducing a whole working framework for a music server just may not be excessively engaging, so for this instructional exercise we will be focussing on Mopidy since it enables us to introduce, without changing the distro. Subsequent to introducing Mopidy, we will introduce Spotify expansion on Raspberry pi to stream tunes from Spotify. More subtleties on Mopidy has been talked about in the past article.

This guide depends on the Raspberry Pi 3 running the Raspbian Stretch OS. I would expect you know about setting up the Raspberry Pi with the Raspbian stretch OS, and you know how to SSH into the Raspberry Pi utilizing a terminal programming like putty or interface the Pi to a Monitor by means of HDMI to boot the Raspbian Stretch work area. In case you have issues with any of this, there are huge amounts of Raspberry Pi Tutorials on this site can help.

Required Components

The main part we requirement for Raspberry Pi 3 Mopidy Server is the Raspberry Pi and all things needed to get it going.

- Raspberry Pi 3 (The guide ought to likewise work for pi 2)

- SD card with Raspbian Stretch pre-loaded

- Ethernet link/Mouse and Keyboard, close by HDMI link to interface with a Monitor

With the SD card embedded, associate the pi to the Monitor through the HDMI link and power the PI. This should boot the pi to the raspbian stretch work area. In case a work area isn't accessible, you can likewise decide to arrangement Raspberry pi in headless mode to do this over SSH or view the Pi's work area from a PC utilizing the VNC Viewer.

When the Pi's work area opens, pursue the means underneath to introduce and arrangement Mopidy on Rpi, and to interface Spotify with Raspberry Pi 3.

1. Install Mopidy in Raspberry Pi

The most effortless approach to introduce Mopidy on stretch is from the Mopidy APT Archive. Utilizing this strategy, Mopidy is consequently refreshed at whatever point the pi is refreshed. To do this pursue the means beneath;

Stage 1: Update the Pi

Of course, we start by refreshing and updating the pi to guarantee everything is cutting-edge and avert similarity issues. To do this, run;

```
Sudo apt-get update

Sudo apt-get upgrade
```

Stage 2: Add the Archive's GPG key

Do this by running;

```
wget -q -O - https://apt.mopidy.com/
mopidy.gpg | sudo apt-key add -
```

The terminal ought to react with "alright"

Stage 3: Add the APT repo to your bundle sources

Next, we add the Mopidy Apt repo to the bundle sources list on the Raspberry Pi. Do this by running;

```
sudo wget -q -O /etc/apt/sources.list.d/
mopidy.list        https://apt.mopidy.com/
stretch.list
```

Stage 4: Run Mopidy Install Command

At last update the Pi, so the new bundle list is enlisted and when the update is finished, introduce Mopidy. Take a note of, a reboot may be essential in the wake of refreshing the pi.

To do this run;

```
sudo apt-get update
```

Pursued by:

```
sudo apt-get install mopidy
```

With this done, you should now have Mopidy introduced on the Pi.

2. Configure Mopidy

Mopidy requires some fundamental design before it very well may be utilized. The degree to which the setup goes in fact relies upon you however there are sure fundamental designs that must be set up.

These designs can either be made physically by running;

```
sudo nano .config/mopidy/mopidy.conf
```

Which will open a clear record for you to begin composing designs, or you experience a simpler option by running the direction;

```
mopidy
```

Following establishment, the direction will naturally create the config record and you would then be able to continue to alter utilizing the past order with the nano proofreader. More on Mopidy design can be found here.

A fundamental alteration to be made to the config document after it has been produced is the arrangement of the http segment of the config record. Changing the port through which the server can be gotten to and setting it to acknowledge association from each hostname/ip.

To do this, run;

```
sudo nano .config/mopidy/mopidy.conf
```

This will open the config document. Look down to the http segment and set its substance to coordinate the picture underneath.

```
[http]
#enabled = true
#hostname = 0.0.0.0
#port = 6680
#static_dir =
#zeroconf = Mopidy HTTP server on $hostname
#allowed_origins =
#csrf_protection = true
```

With that done, spare and close the config record. Our Mopidy is currently prepared for use.

3. Run Mopidy

Mopidy can be run as a help utilizing an init content or by setting it up as a systemd administration. Nonetheless, after establishment and setup, you can run mopidy utilizing;

sudo service mopidy start

This kickstarts mopidy and opens it up to be gotten to by means of any MPD customer. A rundown of customers bolstered by Mopidy can be found here.

Anyway MPD customers are just ready to get to Mopidy if on a similar system and approach the IP address of the server on which Mopidy is introduced. In that capacity you have to acquire the Ipaddress of the Pi. You can do this from the terminal by runing;

```
ifconfig
```

This should show a lot of addresses and your IP address, whenever associated over Wi-Fi it ought to be the one in the area underlined in the picture underneath.

With the IP address got, and Mopidy running, open the program on the pi and enter the IP address pursued by the http port number. This will show you the Mopidy landing page as appeared in the picture underneath.

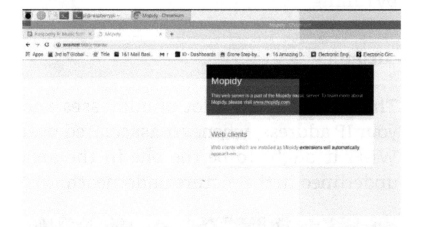

That is it! You would now be able to continue to introduce augmentations, and MPD Clients to oversee Mopidy.

4. Installing Spotify Extension on Mopidy Raspberry Pi 3

Mopidy has many augmentations to assist

clients with overseeing music from numerous stages and utilize different MPD customers. For instance of how to arrangement an augmentation, I will introduce the Mopidy spotify expansion. Spotify is prominent music gushing stage, and to introduce Spotify on raspberry pi pursue the means underneath.

Introduce the augmentation by running;

```
sudo apt-get install mopidy-spotify
```

This will introduce the Spotify on Pi. As referenced before, for each augmentation introduced, you need to include its arrangement subtleties in the mopidy config document. Open the mopidy config document by running;

```
sudo nano .config/mopidy/mopidy.conf
```

At the point when it opens, look to the base of the page and include the accompanying;

> **[spotify]**
>
> **enabled = true**
>
> **username = <your spotify username>**
>
> **password = <your spotify password>**
>
> **client_id = <your client id>**
>
> **client_secret = <your client secret>**

With the end goal that it would seem that the picture underneath.

This, obviously, accept you as of now have a Spotify account as well as in that capacity as of now have a username and secret word. The customer id and mystery is effectively reachable through this connection. Snap on login with Spotify and after you are signed in, the information shows up in the content field.

Spare the config record and leave the nano editorial manager.

Next, we have to introduce spotify-tunigo. This is finished by running;

```
sudo apt-get install mopidy-spotify-tunigo
```

React to any incite during the establishment.

With the establishment complete, we need to include setups for it in the mopidy config record. Open the config document, look to the base and include the lines beneath;

```
[spotify_tunigo]

enabled = true
```

Spare and leave the supervisor.

In conclusion, we have to introduce Mopify, A web customer for Mopidy. Introduce mopify by running;

```
sudo pip install Mopidy-Mopify
```

Next, we add the design for mopify to the mopidy config record. Open the mopidy config document, include the lines underneath, spare and close the supervisor.

```
[mopify]

enabled = true

debug = false
```

With this done, we are presently prepared to arrangement the web customer.

Restart the Mopidy administration to impact every one of the progressions made by running;

> **sudo service mopidy restart**

Invigorate the Mopidy page on localhost that we opened before. It should now resemble the picture underneath with the Mopify augmentation demonstrated.

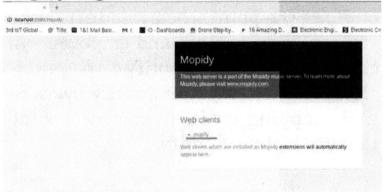

Snap on the mopify content. It should open the mopify window like the picture beneath.

On the mopify window, click on "administrations", it should open a window like the picture beneath. Empower the synchronize administration by essentially tapping on it. At the point when you drift over it you can go to settings and empower synchronization of your Spotify certifications also. Likewise empower Spotify by essentially tapping on it. It may necessitate that you login to Spotify.

With that done, your Raspberry Pi Mopidy Music Server is presently prepared and you can tune in to all the cool tunes on your Raspotify (Raspberry Pi 3 Spotify server). Just indicate the internet browser http://localhost:6680/mopify/you should now observe your tunes recorded as demonstrated as follows.

Hit the play fasten and stream on!

A few other MPD customers exists that can be utilized with Mopidy alongside a few different customers to interface Mopidy to a few music stages.

Conclusion

As referenced as of now, the decision of a media server on the Raspberry Pi begins from choosing if all you need to do with that specific Pi is a media server, or in case you need it to have the option to perform different assignments like home computerization. You will likewise need to choose in the event that you need a music-just media server (music Server) or you need to have the option to deal with a wide range of media. Beside this, the rest is down to feeling and distinguishing which of them normally impacts you.

◆ ◆ ◆

2. DIY RASPBERRY PI GAMING CONSOLE UTILIZING RETROPIE

Raspberry Pi is an astonishing Visa estimated PC generally appropriate for IoT based applications and online servers like Print server, webserver, Media server. Numerous sorts of custom ROMs and custom working frameworks are accessible for Raspberry Pi and you simply need to consume the custom ROM on SD card and addition it in Raspberry Pi. Like Windows 10 and Android can be effectively introduced on Raspberry Pi, check the accompanying connects to know how?

- Step by step instructions to introduce Windows 10 IoT Core on Raspberry Pi

- Introduce Android on Raspberry Pi

So one such mainstream custom OS is RetroPie which is based upon Raspbian OS to transform the Raspberry Pi into a Retro Gaming Console.

RetroPie is a product library used to copy retro computer games on the Raspberry Pi. In this instructional exercise, we will introduce RetroPie on Raspberry Pi and change it into an incredible retro-gaming framework. RetroPie underpins 52 distinctive gaming frameworks that implies you can play everything in one spot. You can without quit a bit of a stretch arrangement RetroPie on your Raspberry Pi by following this instructional exercise.

Components Required

Hardware

- Raspberry Pi
- Secure Digital Card (At least 8GB)
- USB Keyboard
- HDMI Cable
- Monitor

Software

- RetroPie SD Image
- Etcher

Download RetroPie

RetroPie is a product bundle for the Raspberry Pi that depends on the Raspbian OS. To set up RetroPie, Download the most recent RetroPie SD-Card Image from here. There are two adaptations of the RetroPie Secure Digital-Card Image, one for Raspberry Pi Zero and One as well as other for Raspberry Pi 2 as well as 3. You can pick as indicated by your Raspberry Pi adaptation.

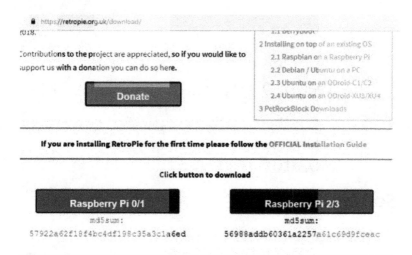

Download Etcher for writing RetroPie Image to SD-Card

balenaEtcher is a free as well as open-source utility used for consuming picture documents, for example, .iso, .img records and zipped envelopes to make live Secure Digital cards as well as USB streak drives. In this instructional exercise, we are utilizing balenaEtcher to consume our Raspbian working framework on our SD card.

You can download Etcher from its official site (https://www.balena.io/etcher/).

It will consequently distinguish your

working framework, or you can pick it physically.

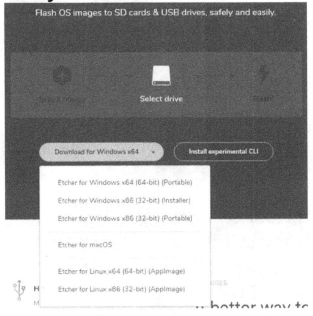

Subsequent to choosing the working framework click on Install exploratory CLI fasten and select Etcher CLI for windows 64 piece (Mine is windows 64 piece, you can pick as per your working framework) and it will begin downloading.

To introduce working framework in SD card, first select the RetroPie SD picture. To choose a picture document, click on Select Image in Etcher. Utilize the record supervisor window and find the picture you unfastened in the past advance. Snap Open and afterward the picture will show up under Select Image. Presently join your SD card to the PC utilizing SD card peruser. Etcher will distinguish it naturally. Etcher won't keep in touch with your hard drives as a matter of course. Presently click Flash to compose the picture record to the Secure Digital card.

Boot Your Raspberry Pi

Supplement the SD card you simply consumed, and different peripherals (Keyboard, HDMI Cable, Game-Controller) at that point turn on the Raspberry Pi. Your Pi will boot now. At the point when it's set, you'll see the screen to set up your controller. In case you have a Game Controller associated arrangement the controls and snap 'alright.' At this point, RetroPie is introduced on your Raspberry Pi.

Presently to arrangement Wi-Fi, pick Wi-Fi from the RetroPie work area and enter your Wi-Fi SSID and Password. After this pick 'Demonstrate IP' to discover your Pi's IP address.

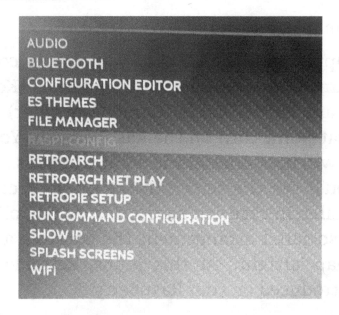

Transfer Game ROMs to Raspberry Pi Gaming Console

After the arrangement, presently move the game ROMs from your Primary PC/Laptop to the Raspberry Pi. You can download ROMs from sites like MAMEDev or ROM Hustler.

Return to the choices page and pick RetroPie Setup from the rundown.

AUDIO

BLUETOOTH

CONFIGURATION EDITOR

ES THEMES

FILE MANAGER

RASPI-CONFIG

RETROARCH

RETROARCH NET PLAY

RETROPIE SETUP

RUN COMMAND CONFIGURATION

SHOW IP

SPLASH SCREENS

WIFI

Pick Manage Packages from the following rundown.

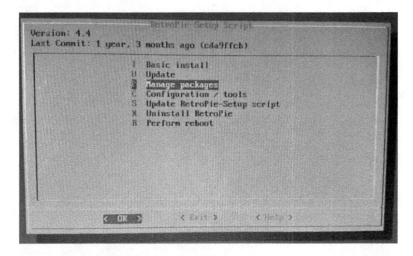

Pick Manage Experimental Packages from the following rundown.

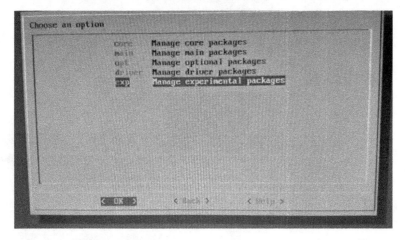

From that point forward, a window with a rundown of utilizations will open, look down, and pick retropie-chief. Feel free to choose Install from source.

Presently you'll see design/choices on the following rundown, pick it, after that pick Enable RetroPie-Manager on boot with the goal that it fires up each time you boot up the Raspberry Pi.

Presently reboot the Raspberry Pi. You can do this by the terminal window or by squeezing the Start button on the RetroPie work area. To open terminal window press F4, at that point type reboot and press the Enter.

After reboot, return to your PC and quest for https://< Your Pi's IP>:8000 utilizing your program. RetroPie director will open on your workstation.

Utilizing this chief window, you can move ROM documents from your workstation to Raspberry Pi.

To move the ROM document click on 'Oversee Rom records for the imitated framework.' Now pick what kind of record you're going to move.

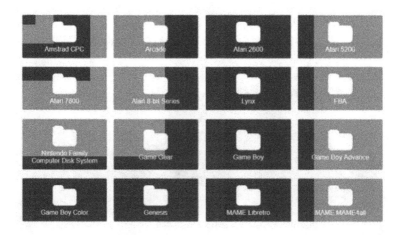

Drag the ROM record or snap in the case to pick the document that you installed from the above-given connection.

At the point when it's set, close the program window and reboot the Pi. At the point when Raspberry Pi boots back up you'll see the Emulation Station program running, and the emulator you transferred a ROM for is presently in the rundown.

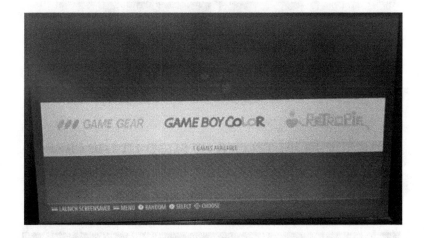

Presently select the emulator and start the game. You can add more games to your RetroPie gaming station by downloading more ROM documents and moving them to Pi.

RetroPie is equipped for imitating countless frameworks. In any case, the quantity of frameworks a Raspberry Pi can process, relies upon the Model of Raspberry Pi. The handling force and RAM of the Raspberry

Pi depend on the model. This implies only one out of every odd variant of the Raspberry Pi will have the option to imitate each framework. For instance, on Raspberry Pi zero you can run Nintendo Entertainment System yet can't hope to run Sega Dreamcast games.

◆ ◆ ◆

3. THE MOST EFFECTIVE METHOD TO ARRANGEMENT DIETPI ON RASPBERRY PI

DietPi on
Raspberry Pi

Raspberry Pi is the pocket estimated PC having practically all the element of an ordinary PC including USB port, LAN port, sound/video yield, HDMI port and so on. There are numerous official and informal outsider working frameworks are accessible for Raspberry Pi and we recently introduced not many of them on Raspberry pi like:

- Introducing Raspbian on Raspberry PI

- Introducing Android on Raspberry Pi

- Introducing Windows 10 IoT on Raspberry Pi

Aside from them, as it has inbuilt Wi-Fi network, Raspberry pi can be utilized to manufacture numerous online servers like Webserver, Media server, Print Server, Plex server and so on.

DietPi is one of the OSes which can be introduced on Raspberry Pi for better and quick execution. As the name proposes, it is a light weighted working framework, and like Raspbian, DietPi is likewise a Debian-based working framework, yet it is path lighter than Raspbian.

DietPi picture document is of approx. 400 MB which is multiple times lighter than Raspbian light. DietPi accompanies 'DietPi-Software' device that has "prepared to run" and enhanced programming for your gadget. Diet Pi programming has several prominent programming like Kodi, Goole AIY, Node-RED, and so on. It has the accompanying highlights:

- DietPi is a very lightweight Debian OS. It is multiple times lighter than 'Raspbian Lite.'

- DietPi is profoundly streamlined for negligible CPU and RAM use, guaranteeing that it can work on any SBC.

- DietPi have an extremely basic interface. It utilizes lightweight Whiptail menus.

- In DietPi, you can rapidly and effectively reinforcement or re-establish your working framework.

- In DietPi you can without quite a bit of a stretch introduce all prominent programming's utilizing 'DietPi-Software'.

Components Required

Hardware

- Raspberry Pi
- Secure Digital Card (At least 8GB)
- USB Keyboard
- HDMI Cable
- Monitor

Software

- Diet-Pi SD Image file
- Etcher

Here, we have utilized a Monitor with Raspberry Pi. Be that as it may, in case you don't have screen, you can arrangement it in headless mode and use SSH to get to it. Become familiar with setting up Raspberry Pi headlessly here without a screen or in the event that you are new to Raspberry Pi, at that point pursue this article to begin with Raspberry Pi.

Download DietPi

You can download the Diet-Pi picture

record from its site; it's allowed to download and utilize it. To download the picture record, explore to https://dietpi.com/#download and click on 'Download.'

Presently select Raspberry Pi and download the picture record. This picture underpins all forms of the raspberry pi.

It will be downloaded as a 7z compress record so utilize 7zip for Windows to un-

fasten it.
Download Etcher

balenaEtcher is a free as well as open-source utility used for consuming picture records, for example, .iso, .img documents and zipped organizers to make live Secure Digital cards as well as Universal Serial Bus streak drives. You can download Etcher from here.

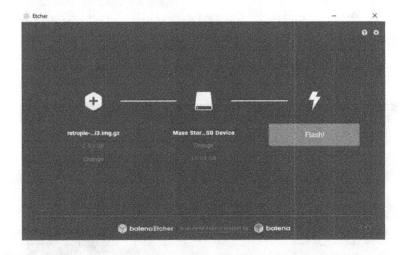

To streak the picture record onto a Secure Digital card select picture document. Presently join your SD card to the PC utilizing SD card peruser. Etcher will distinguish it consequently. Presently click Flash to compose the picture record to the Secure Digital card.

Boot Your Raspberry Pi

Addition the SD card that you simply consumed, and join different peripherals to Raspberry Pi (Keyboard, Monitor, and Mouse) at that point turn on the Raspberry Pi. Your Pi will boot now. At the point when it's set, Log in utilizing the default username and secret key. In the event that you don't have screen the arrangement the Raspberry Pi in headless mode.

Username: root

Secret word: dietpi

After the first login, the Diet pi will naturally refresh the entirety of its bundles, and for that, you need to associate it with the web. You can utilize Ethernet or interface the Pi with Wi-Fi.

To set up Wi-Fi run the accompanying direction in terminal:

dietpi-launcher

After this, a menu with diet pi devices will show up. Select DietPi-Config.

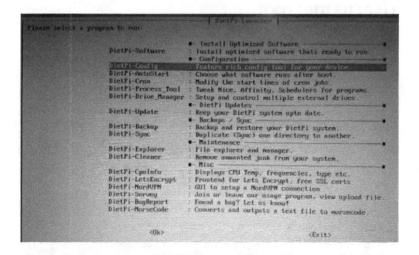

In the following window select 'System Options: Adapters'

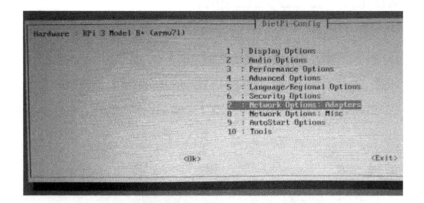

After that select 'Wi-Fi,' at that point check for the accessible systems, pick your system and enter the entrance key/secret word. Presently Diet-Pi is associated with Wi-Fi. Reboot the Pi.

After reboot, it will consequently refresh its bundles. At last, you have a completely working DietPi gadget.

Introduction to DietPi Tools

DietPi has a great deal of helpful Tools. To get to these apparatuses, run the "dietpi-launcher" on an order line utility.

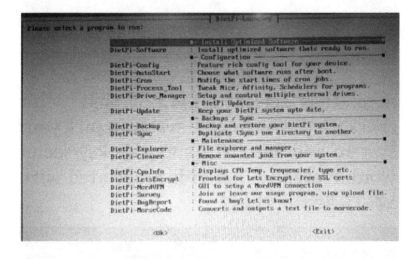

These instruments can be run on a direction line utility as well. Utilize the name of the device as an order; for instance, you can get to DietPi-Software utilizing the accompanying direction:

DietPi-Software

Here's the brisk presentation about every one of the apparatuses beneath.

DietPi-Software

It is utilized to introduce upgraded programming for the DietPi. You can check all the accessible virtual products here.

Dietpi-config

This content is utilized to design equipment and programming settings. Utilizing this device, you can change the Display, Audio, Performance, and Network settings.

Dietpi-autostart

Utilizing this instrument, you can determine how you need your DietPi to boot up.

For instance, you can set your Pi to boot into the work area with Kodi running.

DietPi-Cron

DietPi cron is utilized to change the date and time for beginning each cron work. In the event that you require to run a content at a particular time, put it under the "/and so on/cron.daily/." index and set the time at which you require to run it.

DietPi-Drive_Manager

This instrument is utilized for drive the executives. Utilizing this instrument, you can oversee capacity gadgets, for example, SD card, USB drive, and so forth. You can arrange these gadgets and mount these gadgets with this instrument.

DietPi-Update

Utilizing this device, you can refresh your

DietPi to the most recent form as straight-forward as a single tick.

DietPi-Backup

Utilizing this device, you can rapidly and effectively reinforcement or reestablish your working framework. You can discover the reinforcement documents under the "/mnt/dietpi-reinforcement" catalog.

Dietpi-explorer

This device is utilized to stack a light-weight document administrator and voyager.

DietPi-Cleaner

This apparatus is utilized to tidy up garbage from the working framework. It enables clients to choose the documents to be expelled.

DietPi-BugReport

This apparatus is utilized to send a bug report to DietPi.

So this was a bit by bit instructional exercise about introducing DietPi on Raspberry Pi. I trust this instructional exercise has given you a decent review of DietPi establishment, its highlights and devices.

4. THE MOST EFFECTIVE METHOD TO INTERFACE PCF8591 ADC/DAC ANALOG DIGITAL CONVERTER MODULE WITH RASPBERRY PI

Simple to advanced transformation is a significant errand in installed gadgets, as the majority of the sensors give yield as simple qualities and to sustain them into microcontroller which just comprehend paired qualities, we need to change over them into Digital qualities. So to have the option to process the simple information, microcontrollers need Analog to Digital Converter.

Some microcontroller has inbuilt Analog Digital Converter like Arduino, MSP430, PIC16F877A however some microcontroller don't have it like 8051, Raspberry Pi and so on and we need to utilize some outside Analog to computerized converter ICs like ADC0804, ADC0808. Underneath you can discover different instances of ADC with various microcontrollers:

- How to Use ADC in Arduino Uno?

- Raspberry Pi ADC Tutorial

- Interfacing ADC0808 with 8051 Microcontroller

- 0-25V Digital Voltmeter utilizing AVR Microcontroller

- Instructions to utilize ADC in STM32F103C8

- Instructions to utilize ADC in MSP430G2

- Instructions to utilize ADC in ARM7 LPC2148

- Utilizing ADC Module of PIC Microcontroller with MPLAB and XC8

In this instructional exercise, we will figure out how to interface PCF8591 Analog Digital Converter/Digital-to-Analog Converter module with Raspberry Pi.

Required Components

- Raspberry-pi
- 100K Pot
- PCF8591 ADC Module
- Jumper Cables

It is expected you have Raspberry Pi with most recent Raspbian OS introduced in it and you know how to SSH into the Pi utilizing a terminal programming like putty. On the off chance that you are new to Raspberry Pi, at that point pursue this article to begin with Raspberry Pi. Still on the off chance that you face any issue, at that point there are huge amounts of Raspberry Pi Tutorials that can help.

PCF8591 ADC/DAC Module

PCF8591 is a 8 piece simple to computerized or 8 piece advanced to simple converter module meaning each stick can peruse simple qualities up to 256. It likewise has LDR and thermistor circuit gave on the board. This module has four simple info and one simple yield. It chips away at I2C correspondence, so there are SCL and SDA pins for sequential clock and sequential information address. It requires 2.5-6V supply voltage and have low remain by current. We can likewise control the info voltage by altering the handle of potentiometer on the module. There are likewise three jumpers on the board. J4 is associated with select the thermistor get to circuit, J5 is associated with select the LDR/photograph resistor get to circuit and J6 is associated with select the customizable voltage get to circuit. There are two LEDs on board D1 and D2-D1 shows the yield voltage power and D2 shows the force of supply voltage. Higher the yield or supply voltage, higher the power of LED D1 or D2. You can likewise test these LEDs by utilizing a potentiometer on VCC or on AOUT stick.

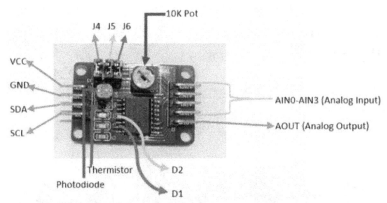

I2C pins in Raspberry Pi

So as to utilize PCF8591 with Raspberry Pi, the main activity is knowing the Raspberry Pi I2C port sticks and arranging I2C port in the Raspberry pi.

The following is the Pin Diagram of Raspberry Pi 3 Model B+, and I2C pins GPIO2 (SDA) and GPIO3 (SCL) are utilized in this instructional exercise.

Designing I2C in Raspberry Pi

Of course, I2C is crippled in Raspberry Pi. So first it must be empowered. To empower the I2C in Raspberry Pi

1. Go to the terminal as well as type sudo raspi-config.

2. Presently the Raspberry Pi Software Configuration Tool shows up.

3. Select Interfacing alternatives and afterward empower the I2C.

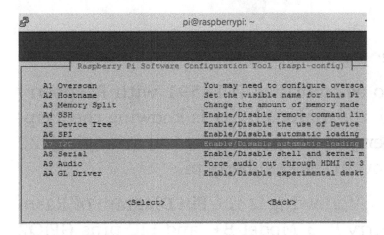

4. In the wake of empowering the I2C reboot the Pi.

Filtering I2C Address of PCF8591 utilizing Raspberry Pi

Presently so as to begin correspondence with the PCF8591 IC, the Raspberry Pi must realize its I2C address. To discover the location initially associate the SDA and SCL stick of PCF8591 to the SDA and SCL stick of Raspberry Pi. Likewise associate the +5V and GND pins.

Presently open the terminal and type beneath order to know the location of associated I2C gadget,

sudo i2cdetect –y 1 or sudo i2cdetect –y 0

In the wake of finding the I2C address now its opportunity to fabricate the circuit and introduce the fundamental libraries for utilizing PCF8591 with Raspberry Pi.

Interfacing PCF8591 ADC/DAC Module with Raspberry Pi

Circuit graph for Interfacing of PCF8591 with Raspberry Pi is basic. In this interfacing model, we will peruse the simple qualities from any of the simple sticks and show it on Raspberry Pi terminal. We can modify the qualities utilizing a 100K pot.

ANBAZHAGAN K

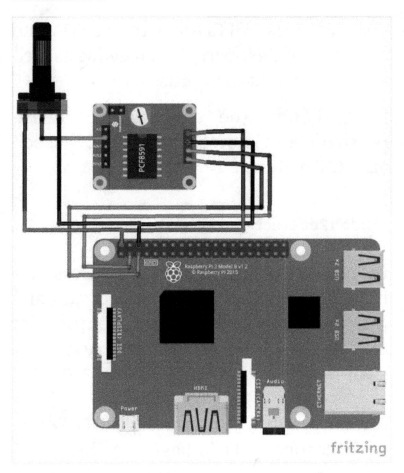

68

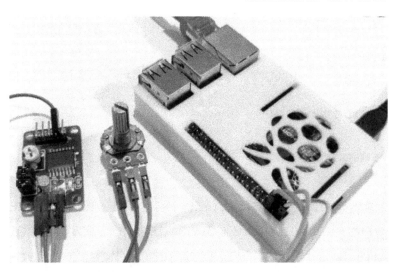

Interface the VCC as well as GND to GPIO2 as well as GPIO of Raspberry Pi. Next, associate the SDA as well as SCL to GPIO3 as well as GPIO5 of separately. At long last associate a 100K pot with AIN0. You can likewise add 16x2 LCD to show ADC values as opposed to demonstrating it on Terminal. Become familiar with interfacing 16x2 LCD with Raspberry Pi here.

Python program for Analog to Digital Conversion (ADC)

Right off the bat, import the smbus library for I2C transport correspondence and time library to give a rest time between printing the worth.

```
import smbus

import time
```

Presently characterize a few factors. The primary variable contains the location of the I2C transport and second factor contains the location of first simple info stick.

```
address = 0x48

A0 = 0x40
```

Next, we've made an object of the capacity SMBus(1) of library smbus

```
bus = smbus.SMBus(1)
```

Presently, in while the principal line advises the IC to make the simple estimation at the main simple info stick. The subsequent line stores the location read at simple stick in a variable worth. At last print the worth.

```
while True:

    bus.write_byte(address,A0)

    value = bus.read_byte(address)

    print(value)

    time.sleep(0.1)
```

Presently at long last spare the python code in some document with .py entension and run the code in raspberry Pi terminal by utilizing beneath direction"

```
python filename.py
```

Before running the code guarantee that you have empowered the I2C correspondence and every one of the pins are associated as appeared in the chart, else it will show mistakes. The simple qualities must beginning appearing on terminal like beneath. Alter the pot's handle, and you will see the progressive change in the qualities. Study running the program in

Complete python code is given underneath.

Code

```
import smbus
import time
address = 0x48
bus = smbus.SMBus(1)
while True:
  bus.write_byte(address,A0)
```

```
value = bus.read_byte(address)
print(value)
time.sleep(0.1)
```

◆ ◆ ◆

5. TRANSFORM YOUR RASPBERRY PI INTO A BLUETOOTH BEACON AND BROADCAST A URL

Raspberry Pi Eddystone Beacon

Bluetooth is a progressive innovation to remotely move the information, control different gadgets, fabricate home mechanization frameworks and so on. However, have you at any point pondered that the Bluetooth can likewise be utilized for broadcasting any data to close by gadgets to show significant data, promotions, simple checkout and so forth. There is a convention created by the Google to play out the undertaking of commercial which can be effectively conveyed in Raspberry Pi to make it Bluetooth Beacon telecaster.

In this instructional exercise we will become acquainted with about (Bluetooth Low Energy) and Bluetooth reference point and introduce the Eddystone Bluetooth Beacon in Raspberry Pi to communicate a URL. Its simple to change over Raspberry Pi into a Bluetooth Beacon as it has inbuilt Bluetooth. What is BLE and Bluetooth Beacon?

The Bluetooth Low Energy, as the name shows devours less power than exemplary Bluetooth. It is accomplished by sending information when required with pre-characterized intermittent updates. Be that as it may, not at all like great Bluetooth it isn't utilized to move Files or Music. A BLE gadget works with Bluetooth V4.0 and can work with low power as a server or as a customer which settles on BLE a perfect decision for signals, shrewd watches, wellness groups and so forth. Great Bluetooth then again is only the straightforward plain old Bluetooth convention that we use to move records and other information. Practically all BLE gadgets have Classic Bluetooth usefulness related with it. We recently clarified BLE in detail with ESP32.

Bluetooth Beacons:

Signals are the equipment gadgets which communicate a few messages to close by hardware gadgets as well as act as a Broadcaster. This innovation empowers the convenient gadgets to play out certain activities when they are in nearness to reference point gadget. Presently, signals can be executed utilizing BLE and exemplary Bluetooth. Since, most cell phones and other electronic gadgets are good with BLE and can be utilized as Beacon recipient so actualizing BLE guide is increasingly effective as contrast with exemplary Bluetooth reference point to diminish control utilization.

On a normal, a Bluetooth Low Energy reference point can transmit BLE sign to 80 meters.
How does BLE Technology works and used with Beacons?

BLE is low power utilization innovation which is intended for short-run correspondence and it is favored where battery life is more significant factor than high information rate. The information move in this correspondence is single direction as it were. BLE signal transmits little information parcels at ordinary interims of time. These information parcels are gotten and decoded by signal scanner application introduced in cell phones. This got information triggers activities like advancing an item or pushing a message.

In Bluetooth signal an ID number is transmitted multiple times each second by the it by means of BLE channels. At that point this ID number is gotten by the Bluetooth empowered gadget and perceived by the reference point scanner application, it joins it to an activity, for example, download an application or bit of substance put away on the cloud, and shows it on the cell phone.
What is Eddystone Beacon?

Eddystone is a convention which is created by Google that permits to communicate one path messages to BLE gadgets. The Eddystone-URL outline frames the foundation of the Physical Web, which helps in disclosure of web content in the encompassing. Reference point can communicate four kinds of information utilizing Eddystone convention. They are as per the following:

- Eddystone-URL for broadcasting URL addresses

- Eddystone-UID for broadcasting reference points IDs

- Eddystone-TLM for broadcasting reference point telemetry like gadget temperature, battery quality, and so forth.

- Eddystone-EID for security.

There are likewise different sorts of signals like iBeacon which is for iOS upheld gadgets, yet Eddystone is just for Android gadgets. Additionally note that Google has suspended Nearby Notifications, presently client should introduce particular guide scanner application that will show the communicated substance.

In this instructional exercise, we will utilize Raspberry Pi as Eddystone Beacon and spotlight on communicating URL address utilizing Eddystone URL so anyone can without quite a bit of a stretch access the communicated data with the assistance of their Android gadgets.

Requirements

Here just Raspberry Pi is expected to assemble this Bluetooth Beacon. It ought to be Raspberry Pi 2 or more current with Raspbian Jessie or a more up to date OD introduced in it.

Here, we will utilize SSH to get to Raspberry Pi on the PC. You can utilize VNC or Remote Desktop association on the workstation, or can interface your Raspberry pi with a screen. Get familiar with setting up Raspberry Pi headlessly here without a screen.
Setup Raspberry Pi for Eddystone Beacon

It is extremely simple to arrangement the Eddystone telecaster on Raspberry Pi. It includes just 3 directions.

This should be possible by designing the HCI (Host controller Interface) which can be get to utilizing hciconfig commad. To check what should be possible utilizing this direction, enter the underneath order in terminal.

hciconfig -h

1. In the first place, we need to Enable the Bluetooth gadget on our Raspberry Pi utilizing underneath direction.

sudo hciconfig hci0 up

2. Presently, we need to Set the Bluetooth to "publicize and not-connectable" gadget utilizing under-

neath direction.

> **sudo hciconfig hci0 leadv 3**

3. Above directions make the gadget to run broadcasting administration, presently simply enter reference point information in next order which contains various edges data and URL in hexadecimal arrangement. Run the underneath direction to begin reference point broadcasting.

> **sudo hcitool -i hci0 cmd 0x08 0x0008 1c 02 01 06 03 03 aa fe 14 16 aa fe 10 00 02 63 69 72 63 75 69 74 64 69 67 65 73 74 07 00 00 00**

To check the communicated message on your advanced cell, download the Physical Web App or Beacon scanner on your Android cell phone and start the filtering. You will see the communicated connection in the application as demonstrated as follows. Snap on the connection to visit and open the site in program.

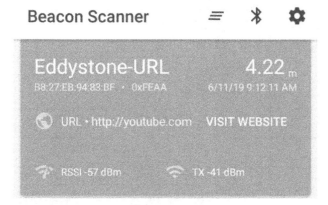

Beacon Scanner

Presently lets comprehend the hexadecimal coding of the message. In beneath table we have given clarification of every single worth present in the code:

Value	Description
0x08	#OGF = Operation Group Field = Bluetooth Command Group = 0x08
0x0008	#OCF = Operation Command Field = HCI_LE_Set_Advertising_Data = 0x0008
1c	Length. The hexadecimal 1c converts to 23 decimal which is the number of bytes that follow.
02	Length
01	Flags data type value

06	Flags data
03	Length
03	Complete list of 16-bit Service UUIDs data type value
aa	16-bit Eddystone UUID
fe	16-bit Eddystone UUID
14	Length. The hexadecimal 14 converts to 15 decimal which is the number of bytes that follow
16	Service Data data type value
aa	16-bit Eddystone UUID
fe	16-bit Eddystone UUID
10	Frame Type = URL
00	TX Power (this should be calibrated)
02	URL Scheme (http:// = 0x02)
63	'c' in hexadecimal
69	'i' in hexadecimal
72	'r' in hexadecimal
63	'c' in hexadecimal
75	'u' in hexadecimal
69	'i' in hexadecimal

74	't' in hexadecimal
64	'd' in hexadecimal
69	'i' in hexadecimal
67	'g' in hexadecimal
65	'e' in hexadecimal
73	's' in hexadecimal
74	't' in hexadecimal
07	.com (.com = 0x07)
00	
00	
00	

To communicate any custom URL utilizing Raspberry Pi Bluetooth Beacon, simply convert the URL characters into hexadecimal utilizing any online device as well as put it in the above direction. Most extreme characters that can be transmitted are 16, in case the URL is excessively long, at that point abbreviate it utilizing any URL shortners administrations like bitly.com and afterward fit the information in above table.

It is awkward and tedious to change over each character into Hexadecimal comparable. So to carry out your responsibility simple there is an Eddystone URL order number cruncher where you simply need to enter URL which you need to be communicated and you will prepare your direction like this.

Eddystone URL command calculator

http://circuitdigest.com

Your commands for "http://circuitdigest.com" are:

$ sudo hciconfig hci0 up

$ sudo hciconfig hci0 leadv 3

$ sudo hcitool -i hci0 cmd 0x08 0x0008 1c 02 01 06 03 03 aa fe 14 16 aa fe 10 00 02 63 69 72 63 75 69 74 64 69 67 65 73 74 07 00 00 00

Bluetooth reference point is presently communicating the URL and working fine yet there is one more thing to be adjusted that is Tx control which is one of the incentive in above order to get the precise good ways from the Bluetooth guide.
Optimize the Transmitting Signal Power by Calibrating Tx Power

In Eddystone outline there are barely any segments which are transmitted and Tx control is one of them which tells the quality of the sign. By translating the quality of the sign, recipient finds the good ways from the Beacon telecaster. The estimation of Tx power can be ranges from - 12 to 10. We need to discover the incentive by hit and preliminary technique to get the precise separation. For this, change the estimation of Tx control in the Eddystone message direction and put your cell phone a ways off of 1 m with Beacon scanner application opened. Presently start putting the estimations of Tx control in the order from 0 to negative qualities. Make sure to change over the decimal qualities in hexa decimal organization, for this utilization the online worth converter instruments for simple interpreting and take the last two digits of the changed over worth. For my situation the hexa esteem is f4. Check the separation in the scanner application, modify the qualities until it shows approx 1m and after that you are to utilize Eddystone URL telecaster with exact separation.

Applications of Eddystone Bluetooth Beacon

Here are a portion of the utilization cases for BLE reference point:

- **BLE empowered retailing:** This innovation can be used to pull in clients in the region of the stores by promoting the energizing offers and deals.

- **BLE reference point empowered occasions:** It can be utilized to simple enlistments at the occasions and in arenas with simple installment checkouts.

- **BLE reference points in Real Estate:** You can get the every one of the subtleties of properties accessible close to you and can book in one touch.

There are many different applications you can consider and actualize as per the necessities.

So this how the Raspberry Pi can be utilized to communicate any message or URL by changing over it into a Bluetooth Beacon utilizing Eddystone.

/>

6. INSTRUCTIONS TO INTRODUCE WHATSAPP ON RASPBERRY PI TO SEND AND RECEIVE MESSAGES

ANBAZHAGAN K

WhatsApp is one of the most famous and broadly utilized informing application yet its accessible for Smartphones and don't chip away at PCs. Be that as it may, there is an approach to introduce it on palm measured PC Raspberry Pi and it works very well utilizing order line interface.

There is a Python library to get to all abilities of an authority WhatsApp on Raspberry pi - Yowsup. It empowers you to utilize your WhatsApp record to trade messages without the first application with your contacts. This library enables the client to make an undeniable custom WhatsApp customer on Raspberry Pi.

Already, it was anything but difficult to introduce

WhatsApp on Raspberry utilizing this library yet from most recent couple of months this library is totally revamped and numerous adjustments have been done in the library, so introducing procedure has gotten more repetitive than previously. Here we will clarify the total procedure of introducing and arranging WhatsApp on Raspberry Pi.

For initiating the WhatsApp on pi, you will require another Phone no. as it won't work with as of now running WhatsApp no. So shockingly for arranging Yowsup regardless we need a telephone and a SIM card, yet after the initial step you can disregard it.

Along these lines, how about we begin.
Requirements

- Raspberry Pi 2 or more current (with Raspbian Jessie or more up to date introduced in it).

- Working Internet Connection

Here, we will utilize SSH to get to Raspberry Pi on the workstation. You can utilize VNC or Remote Desktop association on the PC, or can interface your Raspberry pi with a screen. Become familiar with setting up Raspberry Pi headlessly here without a screen.
Installing Yowsup (WhatsApp) Library in Raspberry Pi

1. First thing that we need to do is refresh and redesign our Pi. It is great practice to refresh the Pi be-

fore introducing any new library or bundle with the goal that you can make certain to have latest library. Run the beneath order to play out the update.

```
sudo apt-get update && sudo apt-get up-
grade
```

Hit 'y' any place request yes/no and hang tight for culmination.

2. Introduce following conditions as required by Yowsup library.

```
sudo apt-get install python-dev lib-
ncurses5-dev
```

```
sudo apt-get install build-essential libssl-
dev libffi-dev python-dev
```

Presently, introduce cryptography bundles (required for encoding the information utilized in WhatsApp) which is now introduced in our Raspberry Pi yet the adaptation isn't perfect as required by Yowsup library.

In this way, introduce required form utilizing beneath direction

pip install cryptography

3. Download the Yowsup library from GitHub utilizing beneath order

git clone git://github.com/tgalal/yowsup.git

4. Go to yowsup index utilizing cd yowsup and introduce the downloaded library utilizing following direction

sudo python setup.py install

5. Presently, we are prepared to arrangement the WhatsApp account. First check whether the library is introduced accurately or not. For this, run the given direction

In the event that you are getting the beneath yield, at that point library is introduced accurately.

Setup WhatsApp Account on Raspberry Pi

In case of introducing WhatsApp on Raspberry Pi, its opportunity to initiate and arrange the WhatsApp on pi.

1. Spare the nation code "cc" and telephone number in a record so that Yowsup customer can get this data for approval. Open nano manager utilizing sudo nano config and spare the data utilizing ctrl+x as demonstrated as follows.

```
sudo nano config

cc=91

phone=91xxxxxxxxxx
```

91 is the cc for India in case you are outside of India utilize your cc and supplant telephone with your telephone number. Ensure the telephone number entered isn't utilized by another WhatsApp account and the SIM card ought to be in telephone from you will get enlistment code in subsequent stage.

2. Presently, register your WhatsApp account utilizing underneath direction.

```
yowsup-cli registration --config config --
requestcode sms
```

Subsequent to running the above order you will get the 6 digit code through a SMS.

3. Utilize that code to enroll the telephone number utilizing the order

> **yowsup-cli registration --config config -- register xxx-xxx**

Supplant xxx-xxx with the code you got on your telephone.

Following a second or two, you'll get a reaction from WhatsApp on the Pi terminal as demonstrated as follows

The reaction contains the secret phrase for your WhatsApp. The ID, appeared by the bolt in above picture, is your secret key without twofold statements. Spare this secret word in the equivalent config document.

Along these lines, open the config document utilizing nano editorial manager and glue the id as

id=***********************

Presently, config document will resemble this. Spare this document.

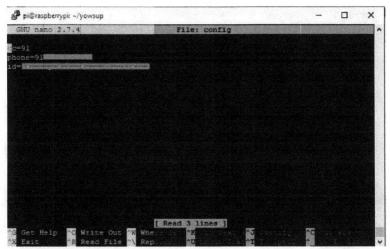

Running the WhatsApp on Raspberry Pi

1. Presently, we are good to go to dispatch WhatsApp on Raspberry Pi. Run the underneath order to begin the WhatsApp.

yowsup-cli demos --yowsup --config config

You will see following reaction from WhatsApp. We need to login now. Enter "/L" and hit enter. For investigating more directions you can type/help.

In the event that you are neglected to login, restart your Raspberry Pi.

2. After login you are good to go to send and get messages.

For sending message to other WhatsApp number sort the accompanying direction.

/message send 91********** "Your message"

Supplant ********** with the beneficiary WhatsApp number. Sent and got messages will be appeared on a similar terminal as demonstrated as follows.

So this is the manner by which the Raspberry Pi can be changed over into a WhatsApp customer to send and get messages from another WhatsApp number. We can likewise actualize the Home Automation utilizing WhatsApp messages yet the Yowsup library isn't working appropriately for that reason and the improvement is proceeding to utilize this usefulness .

/>

7. RASPBERRY PI BLUETOOTH SPEAKER: PLAY AUDIO REMOTELY UTILIZING RASPBERRY PI

Raspberry Pi is a palm estimated PC having in-manufactured Bluetooth, Wi-Fi, Ethernet port, Camera port and so forth which makes it most reasonable microcontroller for IoT based installed applications. It is additionally used to make numerous sort of servers like Print server, Media Server, Web Server and so on. Today we will figure out how a Raspberry Pi can change over a typical speaker having 3.5mm jack into a remote bluetooth speaker.

In this post we will manufacture Raspberry Pi based Bluetooth Speaker by melding the intensity of A2DP, Linux and sound codec to stream the information parcels from a sound source to a sound sink remotely. To do so we are gonna to hack a tad of Linux framework and compose a bit of code in slam and python

and we will be ready to go.
A2DP

A2DP is the abbreviation of Advanced Audio Distribution Profile. This is a convention that is available in practically all the Bluetooth empowered gadgets. It clears route for the information transmission of sound from one gadget to the next gave they are both associated with one another through Bluetooth. A2dp utilizes lossless pressure calculation to pack the sound bundles before transmission to diminish dormancy yet the misfortunes because of this pressure is not really recognizable to human ears.

Preparing Raspberry Pi for Headless Setup

For changing over the Raspberry Pi into a remote Speaker, above all else introduce the OS (Raspbian Stretch) into Raspberry PI SD card, in the event that you are new to Raspberry Pi, at that point pursue this article to begin with Raspberry Pi.

The greater part of us possess a Raspberry Pi and a workstation yet do not have a screen. In any case, so as to SSH into Raspberry Pi we need the equivalent to be associated in a similar system where our PC is associated. We need screen associated with Pi through which we can choose the Wi-Fi and get associated?

All things considered we don't. Raspberry Pi can be associated with Wi-Fi by adding a passage to a record named wpa_supplicant.conf

To do as such, associate the SD card to the PC and open the record rootfs/and so forth/wpa_supplicant/ wpa_supplicant.conf and add the accompanying passage to the equivalent. Remember to open the document with chairman (root) benefits.

```
network={

ssid="wifi_ssid"

psk="wifi_passkey"

key_mgmt=WPA-PSK

}
```

Section should seem to be like this.

```
rocheparadox@brazenparadox: /media/rocheparadox/rootfs/etc/wpa_supplicant
ctrl_interface=DIR=/var/run/wpa_supplicant GROUP=netdev
update_config=1

network={
    ssid= myWifiName
    psk= myPassword"
    key_mgmt=WPA-PSK
}



                                                        8,18        Bot
```

The above section ought to get us associated with the Wi-Fi however that isn't sufficient to make and keep up a SSH association between Raspberry Pi and PC. As a matter of course SSH is impaired in Raspberry Pi, so to empower it, make an unfilled record named ssh in boot registry.

Presently Raspberry Pi is in fact empowered to be gotten to remotely. Associate the raspberry pi to the power source. Presently pi would get associated with the Wi-Fi consequently however its IP address is required so as to SSH into it. There are different ways to discover the equivalent. I use nmap order

nmap -sn [gateway ip address]/24

This order would give us the IP locations of the considerable number of gadgets associated in our system.

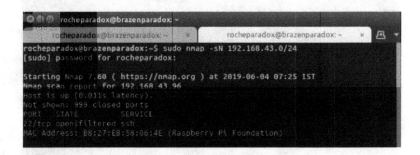

One of them is of raspberry pi's. Presently we realize the IP address of the pi let us interface with the it

ssh pi@pi_ip_address

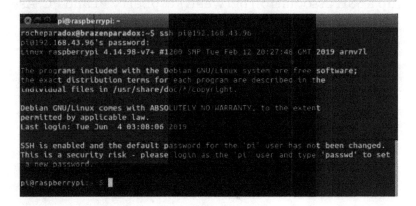

There are additionally different approaches to begin with Raspberry Pi headlessly, check the connection to become familiar with the equivalent.
Prerequisites to be installed in Raspberry Pi

BlueZ

BlueZ is the default application that accompanies Raspbian distro. It is utilized to get to the bluetooth controls of the framework. It can likewise be introduced in case you don't have it accessible in you pi for reasons just you may know.

Underneath order gets the Bluetooth interface application introduced in our pi.

apt-get install bluez

```
pi@raspberrypi: ~
pi@raspberrypi:~ $ sudo apt-get install bluez
Reading package lists... Done
Building dependency tree
Reading state information... Done
The following package was automatically installed and is no longer required:
  bluez-firmware
Use 'sudo apt autoremove' to remove it.
Suggested packages:
  pulseaudio-module-bluetooth
The following NEW packages will be installed:
  bluez
0 upgraded, 1 newly installed, 0 to remove and 92 not upgraded.
Need to get 0 B/721 kB of archives.
After this operation, 3,449 kB of additional disk space will be used.
Selecting previously unselected package bluez.
(Reading database ... 136761 files and directories currently installed.)
Preparing to unpack .../bluez_5.43-2+rpt2+deb9u2_armhf.deb ...
Unpacking bluez (5.43-2+rpt2+deb9u2) ...
Processing triggers for systemd (232-25+deb9u9) ...
Processing triggers for man-db (2.7.6.1-2) ...
Processing triggers for dbus (1.10.26-0+deb9u1) ...
Setting up bluez (5.43-2+rpt2+deb9u2) ...
pi@raspberrypi:~ $
```

PulseAudio

Heartbeat Audio is an application that changes over bytes of PC information into human observation. It is additionally called as the music player. A2DP convention is accessible in PulseAudio application modules.

So let us introduce all the beat sound related applications by utilizing underneath order:

apt-get install pulseaudio-*.

```
pi@raspberrypi: ~
Setting up bluez (5.43-2+rpi2+deb9u2) ...
pi@raspberrypi:~ $ sudo apt-get install pulseaudio-*
Reading package lists... Done
Building dependency tree
Reading state information... Done
Note, selecting 'pulseaudio-module-lirc' for glob 'pulseaudio-*'
Note, selecting 'pulseaudio-dlna' for glob 'pulseaudio-*'
Note, selecting 'pulseaudio-module-raop' for glob 'pulseaudio-*'
Note, selecting 'pulseaudio-module-zeroconf' for glob 'pulseaudio-*'
Note, selecting 'pulseaudio-module-udev' for glob 'pulseaudio-*'
Note, selecting 'pulseaudio-module-jack' for glob 'pulseaudio-*'
Note, selecting 'pulseaudio-module-x11' for glob 'pulseaudio-*'
Note, selecting 'pulseaudio-module-gconf' for glob 'pulseaudio-*'
Note, selecting 'pulseaudio-module-bluetooth' for glob 'pulseaudio-*'
Note, selecting 'pulseaudio-equalizer' for glob 'pulseaudio-*'
Note, selecting 'pulseaudio-esound-compat' for glob 'pulseaudio-*'
Note, selecting 'pulseaudio-utils' for glob 'pulseaudio-*'
The following package was automatically installed and is no longer required:
  bluez-firmware
Use 'sudo apt autoremove' to remove it.
The following additional packages will be installed:
  pulseaudio
Suggested packages:
  pavumeter pavucontrol paman paprefs python-cairo python-rsvg python-gtk2
```

Pairing Bluetooth Device with Raspberry Pi

Open the BlueZ application utilizing the direction

bluetoothctl

A Bluetooth operator is a handle that discussions between two bluetooth empowered gadgets and instate an association between them. There are various sorts of bluetooth operators. The one that we will utilize is NoInputNoOutput operator since it gives us a chance to associate without client mediation. So let us introduce the specialist by running the accompanying directions.

agent NoInputNoOutput

You ought to get the message "Specialist enlisted" as the reaction. Since we have our specialist enlisted, let us make it the default one.

default-agent

For which the reaction ought to be "Default specialist demand fruitful"
Presently let us make our gadget discoverable

discoverable on

For which the reaction ought to be "Changing discoverable on succeeded"

Presently take a stab at interfacing your cell phone or the PC to the Raspberry Pi

Application will provoke us to approve the administrations and we need not do them. Rather we will simply confide in the gadget and associate it. Believing the gadget is significant in light of the fact that when the believed gadget endeavors to associate with the pi, it permits the equivalent with no client mediation at all.

trust [device mac address]

connect [device mac address]

After every one of these activities, your terminal should seem to be like this one.

Yippee! We have our telephone associated with the Raspberry Pi through Bluetooth. However, is that enough? Clearly no, we need our sound information bundles to be moved from the telephone to pi and afterward from the pi to the speaker that is associated with the pi's sound port.

Give us an opportunity to ensure that we have our telephone recorded in the sound wellspring of PulseAudio application by running the beneath order:

pactl list short

It will list all the stacked sound modules, sound sinks and sound sources

Take a gander at the qualities against the sequential number 30. Bluez_source implies the wellspring of sound through BlueZ application which is bluetooth. Cross check the gadget macintosh address which is in the middle of bluez_source and a2dp_source and the location that you have in BlueZ application. For my situation it is bluez-_source.3C_28_6D_FD_65_3D.a2dp_source which is equivalent to the one from the BlueZ application. Presently in case you play a tune from the gadget that is associated with the pi It ought to be steered to the speaker that is associated with the sound port of raspberry pi.

Aha! We have effectively constructed a Bluetooth speaker. We have steered the sound however that isn't all. We can't do all the above advances physically so let us mechanize them utilizing expect content and interface pi with a switch which when squeezed, sets the Pi with gadgets.

Cool? Give us now a chance to get serious.
Automate the Bluetooth Paring Process with Python Scripts

Expect Scripts resemble slam contents yet computerized. It searches for the given word in the terminal and when the equivalent shows up, it sends the order according to the content. Give us a chance to computerize the way toward matching. Make a record called pair_bluetooth_device.expect

```
set timeout 30

spawn bluetoothctl

expect "# "

send "agent off\r"

expect "?gistered"

send "\r"

expect "# "

send "agent NoInputNoOutput\r"

expect "Agent registered"

send "\r"

expect "# "

send "default-agent\r"

expect "Default agent request successful"
```

```
send "\r"

expect "# "

send "discoverable on\r"

expect "Authorize "

send "yes\r"

send "exit\r"
```

Duplicate the code and glue the equivalent in the document. It simply does naturally, the activities that we did while blending the versatile with raspberry pi. It just allows the to gadget interface yet doesn't confide in it. To believe a gadget we need the macintosh address of it. So we will print the yield of this anticipate that content should a log document from which the macintosh address can be held.

```
grep -Pom 1 "(?<=Device ).*(?= Connected)"
```

The above direction prints out the incentive in the center of the string "Gadget" and "Associated". For our situation (Device 3C:28:6D:FD:65:3D Connected: no) it is the macintosh address of the gadget.

Give us a chance to compose an expect content that will take in the macintosh address as the primary contention and trust and associate with that gadget.

Make a record named trust_and_connect.expect

```
set timeout 30

spawn bluetoothctl

expect "# "

send "agent off\r"

expect "?egistered"

send "\r"

expect "# "

send "agent on\r"

expect "Agent registered"

send "\r"

expect "# "
```

```
send "default-agent\r"

expect "Default agent request successful"

send "\r"

expect "# "

send "trust [lindex $argv 0]\r"

expect "Changing"

send "connect [lindex $argv 0]\r"

expect "Connection successful"

send "exit\r"
```

Duplicate the above code into that record. It does the trusting and interfacing part consequently.

Let us currently put this in a Python content document with the goal that the entire blending procedure can be robotized.

Let us a make a document pair_and_trust_bluetooth_device.sh

RASPBERRY PI - NEW TECH

```
cd $(dirname $0)

echo "Pairing..."

expect pair_bluetooth_device.expect > expect_script.log

chmod 777 expect_script.log

sleep 2

echo "Trusting and connecting.."

device_mac_address=$(cat expect_script.log | grep -Pom 1 "(?<=Device ).*(?= Connected)")

echo mac address is $device_mac_address

if [[ ! -z $device_mac_address ]] ; then

        expect trust_and_connect.expect $device_mac_address

else
```

```
        echo "No device connected"

fi

rm expect_script.log
```

So the slam content,

1. Calls an anticipate content (whose yield will be printed to a record named expect_script.log) which,

   1. Starts the NoInputNoOutput specialist

   2. Makes it the default-specialist

   3. Turns on the discoverability of pi

   4. Trusts that somebody will associate and leaves when somebody does or breaks

2. Rest for 2 seconds

3. Get the expect_script.log record for the gadget macintosh address

4. Trusts and interfaces the gadget if the mac_address is invalid

   5. Expels the buildup record expect_script.log
Trigger the Bluetooth Pairing Script with a Button

Presently we have the content to mechanize the matching procedure. Be that as it may, this content needs to run at accommodation, at whatever point the client wants. So lets attach this content with a physical catch so this content gets called each time when catch is squeezed. Hinder is one of the imperative pieces of installed programming. First of all, hinders when detected put the ordinary everyday practice of the program and runs a pre-characterized ISR known as Interrupt Service Routine.

So let us interface the drive catch to gpio stick 11 and dole out an ISR to the equivalent. Inside the ISR, we will call the content.

Give us a chance to make a python record named Bluetooth-speaker-main.py and add the code beneath to it. I have included the remarks in the program so in case that in case you utilize this code, regardless you have them

```
#import required packages

import subprocess

import RPi.GPIO as gpio

import time

import os

import logging
```

```
pair_pin=11

#fetch the file directory from which the
python script is run

fileDirectory          =          os.path.dir-
name(os.path.realpath(__file__))

#Set the log file location as same as the
python script location

logFile=fileDirectory+"/bluetooth-
Speaker.log"

logging.basicConfig(filename=logFile,
filemode='w',  format='%(name)s  -  %
(levelname)s       -       %(message)s',
level=logging.INFO)

def pairNewDevice(channel):

  #ISR for pin 11

  print("Waiting to pair")

  logging.info("Waiting to pair")

  output = subprocess.call(["/bin/bash",-
```

```
fileDirectory+"/pair_and_trust_blue-
tooth_device.sh", ">>", fileDirectory+"/
bluetoothSpeaker.log"])

gpio.setmode(gpio.BOARD)

gpio.setup(pair_pin, gpio.IN, pull_up_
down=gpio.PUD_UP)

try:

  #Set the pair_pin as an interrupt pin
that detects the falling edge and when it

does, call the pairNewDevice function

  gpio.add_event_detect(pair_pin, gpio.
FALLING,        callback=pairNewDevice,
bouncetime=1000)

  print("Bluetooth program has started")

  logging.info("Bluetooth program has
started")

  while True:

    time.sleep(5)
```

```
except KeyboardInterrupt:

  gpio.cleanup()
```

Circuit Diagram

The following is the circuit graph to interface a catch with GPIO 11 of Raspberry Pi to trigger the Bluetooth matching procedure for sound exchange through Bluetooth.

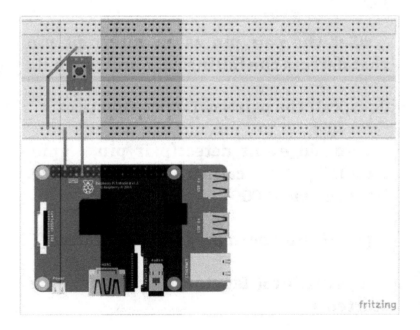

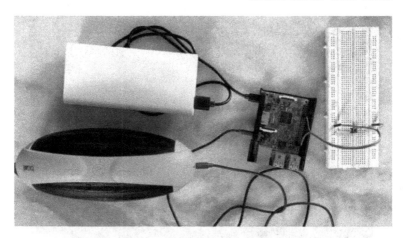

Setup a Cron Job to start the Bluetooth Speaker Python Program on Boot

Presently at long last let us set a cron work which will begin this python program everytime the pi boots up.

```
crontab -e
```

Select your preferred editorial manager and include the underneath line toward the finish of the document

```
@reboot python3 /home/pi/blueooth-speaker/Bluetooth-speaker-main.py
```

ANBAZHAGAN K

```
pi@raspberrypi: ~
# Edit this file to introduce tasks to be run by cron.
#
# Each task to run has to be defined through a single line
# indicating with different fields when the task will be run
# and what command to run for the task
#
# To define the time you can provide concrete values for
# minute (m), hour (h), day of month (dom), month (mon),
# and day of week (dow) or use '*' in these fields (for 'any').#
# Notice that tasks will be started based on the cron's system
# daemon's notion of time and timezones.
#
# Output of the crontab jobs (including errors) is sent through
# email to the user the crontab file belongs to (unless redirected).
#
# For example, you can run a backup of all your user accounts
# at 5 a.m every week with:
# 0 5 * * 1 tar -zcf /var/backups/home.tgz /home/
#
# For more information see the manual pages of crontab(5) and cron(8)
#
# m h  dom mon dow   command
@reboot python3 /home/pi/blueooth-speaker/Bluetooth-speaker-main.py
                                                                15,1
```

This will call our python program each time the pi boots up.

Also, this is it. The hawk has landed. You have made a Headless Raspberry Pi Bluetooth Speaker.

Restart your Pi, pair your telephone and stream the sound. :)

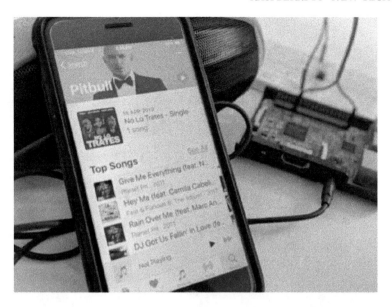

Every one of the contents for this Raspberry Pi Bluetooth Speaker can be downloaded from the GitHub Account.

8. STEP BY STEP INSTRUCTIONS TO QUICKLY SETUP TEAMVIEWER ON RASPBERRY PI

Installing
TeamViewer
on
Raspberry Pi

TeamViewer is the most usually utilized programming to get to the screen of some other PC remotely. It is same as RealVNC yet with more highlights, as in RealVNC you can do content informing and video conferencing while at the mean time getting to the frameworks. TeamViewer is gigantically prominent for giving remote access of your framework to others for investigating or some other work. This application is often utilized by help groups as it makes it parcel simpler to analyze and fix the issues. This is the most ideal approach to deal with the frameworks in case you have numerous clients or various workplaces at various areas as you can deal with every one of your clients from one area.

In this instructional exercise, we will introduce

TeamViewer in Raspberry Pi to get to the its Desktop from anyplace on the planet. It is noticed that standard variant of TeamViewer isn't formally accessible for Raspberry Pi and it is a totally unique procedure to introduce full form in Raspberry Pi. Likewise the full form isn't steady and won't works in some cases. So here we will introduce TeamViewer Host on Raspberry Pi. It is planned uniquely to just get associations from different PCs for example you can't get to others screen from Raspberry Pi yet Raspberry Pi screen can be gotten to from different frameworks.
Requirements

- aspberry Pi 2 or fresher (with Raspbian Jessie or more current introduced in it).

- Working Internet Connection

Here, we will utilize SSH to get to Raspberry Pi on the workstation. You can utilize VNC or Remote Desktop association on the workstation, or can interface your Raspberry pi with a screen. Study setting up Raspberry Pi headlessly here without a screen.
Installing TeamViewer on Raspberry Pi

1. Prior to introducing the TeamViewer, we need to guarantee that our introduced bundles and OS are state-of-the-art. To do this, run the underneath directions individually.

```
sudo apt-get update
```

sudo apt-get upgrade

2. Subsequent to overhauling the bundles on Raspberry Pi, feel free to download the product bundles from TeamViewer server utilizing wget direction. The downloaded record will be a .deb document which is a file document containing all the necessary bundles for TeamViewer.

wget https://download.teamviewer.com/ download/linux/teamviewer-host_arm- hf.deb

3. Presently, introduce the downloaded record utilizing dpkg order.

sudo dpkg -i teamviewer-host_armhf.deb

4. Subsequent to introducing, there will be a few blunders about bundles not being introduced appeared on terminal. We need to fix these blunders utilizing bundle director to fix the documents. Run the accompanying order to fix the mistakes.

sudo apt --fix-broken install

```
dpkg: error processing package teamviewer-host (--install):
 dependency problems - leaving unconfigured
Processing triggers for gnome-menus (3.13.3-9) ...
Processing triggers for desktop-file-utils (0.23-1) ...
Processing triggers for mime-support (3.60) ...
Processing triggers for hicolor-icon-theme (0.15-1) ...
Errors were encountered while processing:
 teamviewer-host
pi@raspberrypi:~ $
```

5. Presently, if TeamViewer is introduced and running on Raspberry Pi appropriately. It will be consequently start with each boot of Raspberry Pi. So you don't have to begin it physically utilizing directions. Configuring TeamViewer on Raspberry Pi

1. Presently, we need to arrangement a secret word for TeamViewer. It tends to be arrangement either by utilizing order line or utilizing GUI. On terminal, it very well may be finished utilizing underneath order

sudo teamviewer passwd <password>

Keep your secret word secure as it can enable somebody to get to your Pi on the off chance that they get your TeamViewer ID.

2. Subsequent to setting up secret word, we need TeamViewer ID to make the association between Raspberry Pi and the framework. To get the TeamViewer ID , run the underneath direction

teamviewer info

Spare the ID some place, we will require it when we associate Raspberry Pi with the framework.

3. At the mean time, in case you have TeamViewer account, at that point you can get the entrance effectively without setting secret key or ID.

Run the underneath direction and enter your accreditations.

sudo teamviewer setup

You will be approached to acknowledge permit understanding, pursue the means as appeared on the screen and enter your certifications. In case you are utilizing GUI for arrangement, click on TeamViewer symbol on taskbar.

In case you need to depend on TeamViewer ID, at that point click on set an individual secret key or in case you need to get a simple access, at that point feel free to tap on Grant simple access and enter your Team-Viewer certifications.

Presently, we are prepared to get to the Raspberry Pi remotely from PC.
Connecting with Raspberry Pi remotely using Team-Viewer

1. To get the entrance of Raspberry Pi on other frame-work we need to introduce TeamViewer program-ming in it. Along these lines, download the product from this connection and introduce it.

2. Open the TeamViewer in PC and you will see the accompanying window. Presently, you need to enter the TeamViewer ID of Raspberry Pi in Partner ID space.

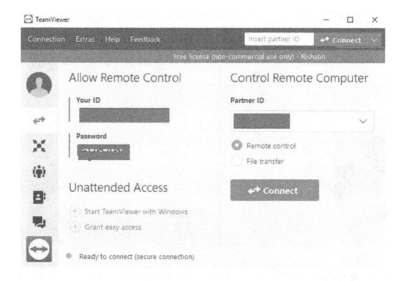

3. Enter the TeamViewer ID of Raspberry pi and snap on associate. At that point it will request secret word that you have set in Raspberry pi, enter the secret key and snap OK. In case every one of the settings are right, at that point you will see Raspberry Pi work area in a window as appeared.

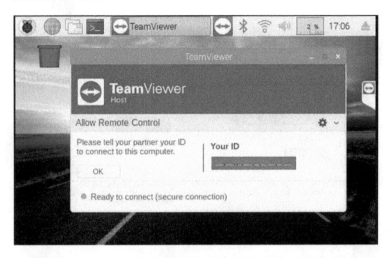

4. Presently, you can control and access every one of the documents of your Raspberry Pi remotely and can likewise visit with the other client as demonstrated as follows.

This is the way we can get to the Raspberry Pi work

area remotely by introducing the TeamViewer have bundle in Raspberry Pi.

◆ ◆ ◆

9. INTRODUCING MACHINE LEARNING SOFTWARE TENSORFLOW ON RASPBERRY PI

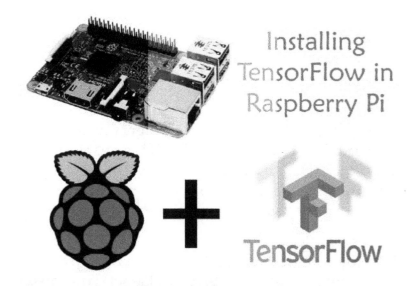

AI and Artificial Intelligence are the slanting themes in the enterprises now days and we can see their expanding inclusion with the dispatch of each new hardware gadget. Pretty much every utilization of Computer science designing is utilizing Machine Learning for breaking down and foreseeing the future outcomes. As of now, there are numerous gadgets abounded in the market that are utilizing the intensity of Machine learning as well as Artificial Intelligence, similar to Smartphone's camera utilizes AI empowered highlights for face identification and telling the clear age from the face discovery.

There is nothing unexpected that Google is the pioneers in this innovation. Google previously made numerous ML and AI systems that we can without much of a stretch actualize in our applications. TensorFlow is one of the outstanding Google's open source Neural Network library which is utilized in AI applications like Image order, object discoveries, and so on.

In forthcoming years, we will see more utilization of AI in our day by day life and AI will have the option to deal with your day by day assignments like requesting basic food item web based, driving a vehicle, control your home machines and so forth. Along these lines, why we abandoned to abuse some machine calculations on versatile gadgets like Raspberry Pi.

In this instructional exercise, we will find out how to introduce TensorFlow on Raspberry Pi and will give a few models with basic picture characterization on a pre-prepared neural system. We recently utilized Raspberry Pi for other Image Processing undertakings like Optical Character Recognition, Face Recognition, Number Plate Detection and so on.
Requirements
- Raspberry Pi with Raspbian OS introduced in it (Secure Digital card atleast 16 GB)

- Working Internet Connection

Here, we will utilize SSH to get to Raspberry Pi on the PC. You can utilize VNC or Remote Desktop association on the PC, or can interface your Raspberry pi with a screen. Study setting up Raspberry Pi headlessly here without a screen.

Raspberry pi, being a versatile and less power devouring gadget, is utilized in some continuous picture preparing applications like Face Recognition, object following, Home security framework, Surveillance camera and so on. Any by utilizing any Computer Vision programming like OpenCV with Raspberry Pi, parcel of amazing picture handling applications can be assembled.

In past, introducing TensorFlow was a serious troublesome activity however late commitment of ML and AI engineers made it exceptionally basic and now it very well may be introduced just by utilizing hardly any directions. In case you know a few nuts as well as bolts of Machine learning and profound learning it will be useful for you to know whats going inside the neural system. Be that as it may, regardless of whether you are new to Machine learning area, there will be no issue you can in any case proceed with the instructional exercise and utilize some model projects to learn it.

Installing TensorFlow in Raspberry Pi

The following are the means for introducing Tensor-Flow in Raspberry pi:

Stage 1: Before introducing TensorFlow in Raspberry Pi, first refresh and overhaul the Raspbian OS by utilizing following directions

```
sudo apt-get update

sudo apt-get upgrade
```

Stage 2: Then Install the Atlas library to get support for the Numpy and different conditions.

> **sudo apt install libatlas-base-dev**

Stage 3: Once that is done, introduce TensorFlow through pip3 utilizing beneath direction

> **pip3 install tensorflow**

It will take some to introduce the TensorFlow, in the event that you face some mistake while introducing, simply retry it utilizing above direction.

Stage 4: After effective establishment of TensorFlow, we will check whether it is introduced appropriately by utilizing a little Hello world program. To do that Open nano content manager utilizing underneath direction:

```
sudo nano tfcheck.py
```

What's more, Copy-glue beneath lines in nano terminal and spare it utilizing ctrl+x and hit enter.

```
import tensorflow as tf

hello = tf.constant('Hello, TensorFlow!')

sess = tf.Session()

print(sess.run(hello))
```

Stage 5: Now, run this content in the terminal utilizing underneath direction

```
python3 tfcheck.py
```

In the event that every bundles introduced appropriately, at that point you will see a Hello Tensorflow! message in last line as demonstrated as follows, overlook every one of the admonitions.

ANBAZHAGAN K

```
File Edit Tabs Help
pi@raspberrypi:~ $ python3 tfchck.py
.../lib/python3.5/importlib/_bootstrap.py:222: RuntimeWarning: compiletime vers
3.4 of module 'tensorflow.python.framework.fast_tensor_util' does not match
:ime version 3.5
 :turn f(*args, **kwds)
 ../lib/python3.5/importlib/_bootstrap.py:222: RuntimeWarning: builtins.type si
 :hanged, may indicate binary incompatibility. Expected 432, got 412
 :turn f(*args, **kwds)
 :llo, TensorFlow!'
```

It works fine and now we will accomplish something fascinating utilizing TensorFlow and you don't have to have any information on Machine learning and profound figuring out how to do this undertaking. Here a picture is encouraged in a pre-fabricated model and TensorFlow will distinguish the picture. TensorFlow will give the closest likelihood of what is in the picture.

Installing Image Classifier on Raspberry Pi for Image Recognition

Stage 1:- Make an index and explore to the catalog utilizing beneath directions.

mkdir tf

cd tf

Stage 2:- Now, download the models which is accessible on TensorFlow GIT store. Clone the storehouse into the tf catalog utilizing beneath order

git clone https://github.com/tensorflow/models.git

This will set aside some effort to introduce, and it is

huge in estimate so ensure you have adequate infor-mation plan.

Stage 3:- We will utilize picture order model which may be found in models/instructional exercises/pic-ture/imagenet. Explore to this envelope utilizing be-neath order

```
cd models/tutorials/image/imagenet
```

Stage 4:- Now, feed a picture in the pre-manufactured neural system utilizing underneath direction.

```
python3 classify_image.py --image_file=/
home/pi/image_file_name
```

Supplant image_file_name with the picture that you require to sustain and afterward hit enter.
The following are a few instances of distinguishing and perceiving pictures utilizing TensorFlow.

TensorFlow Detecting Cellular phone
with almost 99% accuracy

TensorFlow Detecting Cat Image

Not terrible! the neural net characterized the picture as an Egyptian feline with a high level of sureness when contrasted with different choices.

TensorFlow Detecting Mountain Valley with 65% probability of Alp

In all the above models, results are quite great and the TensorFlow can undoubtedly characterize the pictures with the nearby conviction. You can attempt this utilizing your tweak pictures.

On the off chance that you have some information on Machine adapting, at that point it can perform Object recognition on this stage utilizing a few libraries.

10. STEP BY STEP INSTRUCTIONS TO INTRODUCE ANDROID ON RASPBERRY PI

Android on
Raspberry Pi

The prominent working framework utilized in Raspberry Pi is Raspbian which is a linux based authority OS for Raspberry Pi, utilizing which we have manufacture numerous Raspberry Pi Applications. We can without much of a stretch introduce Linux and Windows working frameworks on Raspberry Pi, yet because of the absence of legitimate help from Android, introducing Android on Raspberry Pi has never been that simple. Some altered Android OS is accessible that supports Raspberry Pi yet never work like the first Android. However, in case regardless you need to introduce and utilize Android on the Raspberry Pi, there are a portion of the outsider Android OS like emteria.OS, LineageOS, Custom Android 7.1 form, Android Things are accessible.

Today we will change over the Raspberry Pi in an Android gadget utilizing a prominent stage - emteria.OS. Installing Android on a Raspberry Pi 3 using Emteria OS

Emteria.OS is a full form of Android for Raspberry Pi. It's Free to use during the underlying arrangement with certain impediments, however in case you require to utilize it for the mechanical reason, you'll need to initiate your gadget with an authorized rendition. Picking a free form will enable you to proceed with emteria.OS and use it for nothing. There are some restrictions like it will reboot after like clockwork, and has a watermark in the corner. For the testing reason, it is great, however on the off chance that you need to utilize it on the modern level, you need to purchase an authorized form of it.

Emteria OS depends on RTAndroid, and this variant is progressively appropriate for business employments. Emteria is making arrangements for individual use forms sooner rather than later.

Here is the bit by bit control for introducing Emteria OS:

Stage 1: Register on emteria.com

To download the emerita OS installer, you'll first need to enroll a record on emteria official site. To do so explore to emteria.com, in the upper right corner click on 'Register' and fill your own subtleties, after that affirm your email address, and afterward make sign into the emteria.OS site.

Stage 2: Download the installer

Presently on emteria site click on 'downloads' and download the emerita OS installer for windows and afterward introduce the installer. This installer will streak the SD picture document of emteria.OS onto a SD card.

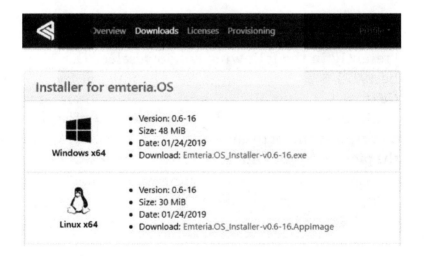

Presently run the installer and enter your emteria.OS username and secret word, at that point click on

'Login.'

Stage 3: Flash the SD Card

Presently in the following window, select the Raspberry Pi 3 as your gadget for introducing the OS. Next, select your SD card as the establishment area and afterward hold up till the installer download the picture document of emteria Os and afterward streak the picture to your microSD card.

Hold up till the procedure finishes, after that nearby the Installer and securely evacuate the microSD card. At that point embed the SD card in your controlled off Raspberry Pi 3. Associate a showcase, console, mouse, and afterward control it up.

Presently Android will boot. This will take some time. After this, you should see the accompanying screen. Snap on next in the base right corner.

In up and coming windows, select the Language, Time-Zone and set the Wi-Fi organize.

From that point onward, the home screen of Emteria OS should begin as demonstrated as follows

Presently the Android working framework is introduced on Raspberry Pi.
Running Android apps on Raspberry Pi

Presently, as Android is running on your Raspberry Pi, you can introduce some applications. In authentic Android Play Store is utilized to introduce applications, however in Emteria OS, you can introduce applications effectively utilizing F-Droid.

From home screen open the F-Droid application. It works also to the play store. Like the Play Store, there are various classifications for various applications. You can likewise look for applications that you need to introduce.

Select the application you need to introduce, at that point click on the introduce button.
Sideloading Android apps on Raspberry Pi

Some Android application that isn't on F-Droid can be

introduced utilizing the APK document. In case you require to introduce Netflix, download the apk utilizing the emteria OS program.

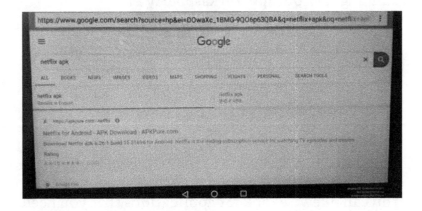

In the wake of downloading the APK, introduce it. Presently you are prepared to utilize Netflix on your Raspberry Pi.

Different Android OS available for Raspberry Pi

There is no official Android OS for Raspberry Pi, yet

at the same time, some Android OS is accessible for Raspberry Pi. Here are the absolute best choices accessible:

1. Emteria OS

Utilizing emteria OS, you can without quit a bit stretch introduce the Android-put together working framework with respect to the Raspberry Pi right away. Emteria.OS is a full form of Android accessible for Raspberry Pi. There is three variants of emteria OS: Evolution, Personal, and Business adaptation. Advancement variant is allowed to utilize, yet with certain restrictions while for the individual and business form, you need to pay per gadget.

The present variant of emteria OS is basically for organizations employments. In businesses, you can utilize emteria OS from candy machines and advanced signage to the point of offer and mechanical control gadgets.

2. LineageOS

Heredity OS doesn't formally bolster the Raspberry Pi, however a few people modified it for the Pi 3B and Pi 3B+. Current Lineage OS adaptation is 15.1, which depends on Android Oreo 8.1.

The Lineage OS is for cutting edge clients just, as it requires specialized information to set it up and to introduce applications. Google Play Store isn't introduced naturally. Yet at the mean time, you can introduce the Android applications utilizing APKs.

3. Android Things

Android Things isn't the correct decision for most clients, as this Android Things OS is unique in relation to the form of Android found on tablets and telephones.

Android Things is essentially utilized for creating Internet-associated machines and other IoT gadgets, and it just enables the client to run a solitary Android application at once. It's much more shortsighted than full Android, and you have to program it from a different PC. You can use the Android studio for programming your gadgets.
4. Custom Android

There is some custom rendition of Android is likewise accessible; for instance, Android 7.1, Android 8.1, and Android 9 Pie. In the event that you're actually capable, at that point you might require to evaluate these Android TV and Android tablet forms of Android on the Raspberry Pi 3. Be that as it may, these custom adaptations accompany a sprinkling of applications, and you ought to hope to experience strength issues.

In case you're searching for creating Internet-associated machines and other IoT gadgets utilizing Android, at that point use Android Things generally for business Android support on Raspberry Pi 3, you can attempt emteria.OS. The Evaluation form of emteria.OS is allowed to utilize however as told earlier, this variant has a few restrictions, yet you will have the option to use for some universally useful applications and make sense of how great it performs before you get it.

/>

Thank You !!!